NEW TESTAMENT ARCHAEOLOGY

JOHN McRAY

Contents

Kregel
Publications

The Role and Method of Archaeology

Archaeology's contribution

Archaeology has contributed in a number of significant ways to the study of the New Testament.

1. *Archaeology has enlightened our understanding of some of the geographical settings in which biblical events occurred.* One example of this is the city of Jericho. Luke says Jesus healed a blind man as he was going into the city (Luke 18:35); but Mark says that this event occurred when Jesus was leaving the city (Mark 10:46). Excavations have revealed that Herod the Great built a new section of Jericho four miles south of the older city. Thus, Jesus was going out of one area and into another one when he healed Bartimaeus.

Above: Excavated site of Qumran seen from a cave in a cliff beside the Dead Sea.

Below: Excavations at Qumran.

Measuring elevation in a baulk (wall of a trench in an excavation).

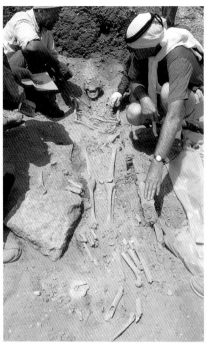

Excavating skeletons buried under a building.

2. *Archaeological excavation has contributed to our understanding of the religious background of the New Testament world.* For instance, discoveries of many ancient books of religious sects at Nag Hammadi, Egypt, and in the settlement known as Qumran near the Dead Sea, Israel, have provided information about heresy in the early church and about the early stages of the formation of the New Testament.

3. *Results of archaeological excavations have helped prevent the New Testament from being 'mythologized', by keeping it in the realm of history and historical geography.* An example of this is the affirmation of the credibility of the Gospel of John by the discovery in Jerusalem of the Pool of Bethesda (John 5:2) and the Pool of Siloam (9:7). Similarly, the name of Pilate (John 19:13) has been found on a stone in the Roman theatre at Caesarea, and the name of Erastus (Romans 16:23) can be seen on an inscription in the stone pavement near the large theatre in Corinth, Greece. Gallio (Acts 18:12) left an inscription with his name on it at Delphi in Greece and the name of Quirinius (Luke 2:2) has been found on an ancient coin. Even though such discoveries do not 'prove' the New Testament to be the Word of God, they do put these scriptural names and places into the stream of historical geography.

4. *Archaeological excavation has produced many documents which are extremely important in reconstructing and affirming the reliability of the biblical text.* Some of the most recent and important examples of this are Egyptian papyri, such as those known as Oxyrhynchus, Chester Beatty, Bodmer and Rylands. These portions of the New Testament text, written in Greek and dating from the late first to the mid-third centuries, have significantly altered our understanding of the Greek text, as we will see later.

An archaeological discovery seldom bears so directly on the text of an ancient document that it may be said specifically to confirm or refute that text. Archaeology cannot prove the New Testament either to be theologically inspired or historically

Reading (evaluating) pottery discovered in an excavation.

Top: Using Ground Penetrating (Sub-surface interface) radar.

Bottom: Cleaning excavated pottery.

accurate; but scripture does not need confirmation of its theological truths and historical references in order to produce faith in the hearts of its readers (John 20:30–31) – for which purpose it was written.

The excavation and identification of such New Testament sites as Corinth, Philippi, Thessalonica, Ephesus, Caesarea, Capernaum, Jericho and Samaria have greatly increased our knowledge of these ancient sites and their historical settings, illuminating our understanding of events described in the Bible text.

A legitimate study

While there is no archaeological methodology peculiar to the Bible, the same is true of the classics. If we may legitimately consider classical archaeology to be a 'field of inquiry', the same may be said of 'biblical archaeology', which exists, not as a separate discipline, but as a field of inquiry utilizing the general disciplines of the field of archaeology. It is as valid to excavate Corinth to discover its relation to the New Testament as to discover its relation to the Peloponnesian wars of classical history. To refer to such an excavation as either biblical or classical would be to describe the field of inquiry – not the discipline or the methodology.

Scientific tools

Modern scientific technology makes excavation methodology more precise. Carbon 14 is used to provide dates for organic material uncovered, while potassium argon dating is used for the much older inorganic materials. Neutron activation analysis can determine the origin of the clay used in pottery found in excavation. Both ground and aerial photogrammetry are now being used to produce extremely accurate three-dimensional drawings of baulks, tomb facades and other structures as well as to produce more accurate maps. Magnetometers and resistivity instruments locate underground discontinuities in much the same way as radar overground. Infrared photography can locate stone beneath the ground by recording the difference between the amount of heat given off by such stones and by the soil around them.

Civic, Religious and Domestic Structures

The forum
Cities of the New Testament period customarily consisted of square city blocks, built around a rectangular central public area, called a 'forum', by the Romans, and an 'agora', by the Greeks. In and around this area stood many civic structures important to the life of the community. The forum was surrounded by small stone shops, hence the usual term 'marketplace' to refer to this large open area.

Theatre
Near the forum it was customary to build a theatre, which was used not only for the performance of plays, musical productions and other kinds of entertainment, but also for civic gatherings. The theatres were constructed of stone, with tiered seating looking down on to the stage, which had a wall behind it reaching to the same level as the top row of seats. Some theatres were built into the side of a hill, others on level ground, but all were built in a semi-circular pattern, which enhanced the sound of the actors' voices.

Latrines and baths
Close to the forum would be a public latrine, with toilet seats carved into stone benches along its sides. A bathhouse was usually built nearby, providing not only facilities for public bathing, but also a place for exercise. Each bathhouse had a changing room, plus three rooms for experiencing progressively cold, warm and hot baths.

Offices
Also often close to the forum area were offices of civic importance, such as the senate building in Rome, and in Ephesus the office of the town clerk who stopped a public riot in the theatre adjacent to his office (Acts 19:35–41).

Temples
Cities of the New Testament era normally also had various religious structures.

Greek and Roman temples, dedicated to various gods, were built near the forum. These temples were built of stone, with columns in the Doric, Ionic or more ornate Corinthian order, and were attractive and prominent features of a city. In Corinth, seven Doric columns of the Temple of Athena still stand adjacent to the forum.

In Athens, the Temple of Athena, better known as the Parthenon, still stands on the Acropolis, above the commercial and civic forums, it consisted of a single circle of columns supporting a roof. Only a few metres east of the Parthenon, and less well known, but more significant for Paul and the early church, was the Temple of Rome and Augustus. It was built soon after 27 B.C., and is identified from a dedicatory inscription that may still be seen, lying at the site. With its dedication to the goddess Roma and to the emperor Augustus, this temple underlines the importance of emperor worship in the New Testament period.

At the western extremity of the forum in Corinth, a huge temple was built in the reign of Tiberius or earlier, probably to house the Imperial Cult, testifying to the shift during the first century A.D. from worship of the Olympian gods to worship of the Emperor.

Top: Stone shops in agora in Ephesus.

Bottom: Latrine in Ephesus.

Top: Bathhouse in Herculaneum.

Bottom: Atrium of a house in Ephesus.

was not until the time of the emperor Constantine (306–337) that Christians were allowed to build church buildings. Almost 200 Byzantine church buildings, dating from the first half of the fourth century until the beginning of the eighth, have been found in excavations in the Holy Land; many others have been discovered throughout the Mediterranean world.

Housing

Domestic architecture in the early Christian world varied considerably between rural areas and the cities. In the villages, small houses were usually built of mud and stone, and poor people slept on straw mats or animal-skin rugs, usually on floors of beaten earth.

In cities such as Ephesus and Rome, there were large apartment buildings as well as Roman-style houses. However, in fourth-century Rome, there was only one private house for every 26 blocks of apartment houses. The poor in large cities of the empire lived in tenements, which strongly resembled the large, plain apartment buildings in Rome today.

The better-off built private houses containing small bedrooms with beds with wooden or bronze frames, laced with ropes on which sleeping mats were laid. In Pompeii and Herculaneum, these beds usually occupied one end of the bedroom, reaching from wall to wall. Most beds were single, but married couples used double beds. Couches (*triclinia*) for three (sometimes six) were found in the dining rooms of some of the wealthy.

Synagogues

The synagogue was both the religious and the cultural and social centre of the Jewish community in cities of the first three centuries A.D. More than 100 have been found in Israel, more than half of which are in Galilee and the Golan Heights. Of the 50 and more that have a shape that is still visible, no two are identical in size or interior plan. The number of synagogues was determined by the size of the Jewish population; large cities often had many synagogues. Early Jewish sources claim that Jerusalem had more than 300.

Most synagogues excavated at the present time date to the third and fourth centuries A.D., but some dating to the first century have been discovered at Herodium, Masada and Gamla. In the first two centuries A.D. synagogue congregations, like those of the church, normally met in private homes.

Churches

Since Christianity was not a legal religion at the time of the early Roman Empire, the church could not own property. References in the New Testament to Christian meeting places imply that believers met in homes or rented rooms (see for example 1 Corinthians 16:19; Romans 16:5; Philemon 2; Colossians 4:15). It

Herodian Jerusalem in the Time of Jesus

The Temple Mount

Herod the Great (37–4 B.C.), who was king in Judea at the time of Jesus' birth, was involved in many building projects throughout the country. His best-known projects are associated with the Temple Mount in Jerusalem. The basically rectangular platform forming the Temple Mount today represents the area renovated by Herod, which doubled the size of the original Temple grounds. The Muslim Dome of the Rock stands in this space today, probably on the very spot where the Jewish Temple once stood.

Archaeological remains of Herod's building programme are preserved in several places on the Temple Mount. Some Herodian stones still remain in the wall of the south-eastern section, today called 'the pinnacle of the Temple', where Jesus was tempted by Satan (Luke 4:9). Portions of the original Double Gate and the Triple Gate are also preserved in this wall, and excavations have revealed a 6.5 metre- (21 foot-) wide stone pavement that Herod built in front of these gates.

Wide steps descended 6.75 metres (22 feet) southwards from these gates to a plaza. Pools, plastered cisterns and *mikvaot* (Jewish ritual baths) have been excavated in this area. They were used for individual purification by the large crowds of Jewish pilgrims who gathered here before entering the Temple courts to worship. These pools may also have been used to immerse the 3,000 new believers on the Day of Pentecost (Acts 2:38–41).

A stone pavement has also been excavated, running north along the western wall of the Temple Mount. Today 26 courses of the original Herodian stone still stand in this wall, 7 of them above ground and 19 underground.

Temple inscriptions

Two stone slabs have been found containing inscriptions that originally hung on a small balustrade wall between the Court of the Gentiles and the Temple itself. The text reads:

> NO FOREIGNER IS TO ENTER WITHIN THE FORECOURT AND THE BALUSTRADE AROUND THE SANCTUARY. WHOEVER IS CAUGHT WILL HAVE HIMSELF TO BLAME FOR HIS SUBSEQUENT DEATH.

Paul was erroneously assumed to have taken Trophimus the Ephesian

Top: Pool south of the Pinnacle of the Temple.

Bottom: Excavation area south of the Pinnacle of the Temple.

Top: One of the mikvaot excavated south of the Pinnacle.

Bottom: Pavement beside western wall.

(a Gentile) beyond this wall into the inner Jewish courts (Acts 21:29).

Herod's palace
As part of his western palace in Jerusalem, Herod built three large towers, which he named after friends and relatives: Hippicus, Phasael and Mariamne. The lower part of one of the towers, generally regarded as Phasael, still stands intact at the modern Jaffa Gate into the Old City.

An inscription, believed to be the first New Testament text carved in stone yet discovered, and one of the earliest New Testament quotations ever found, was found in 2003 in the Kidron Valley near the south-east corner of the Temple Mount, on the wall of a tomb commonly (but mistakenly) called Absalom's Tomb. The text is Luke 2:25; it refers to Simeon, the man who held the baby Jesus when he was brought to the Temple for the ceremony of Mary's purification.

Herodian gate
In the northern wall of the Old City of Jerusalem, a gate has been discovered located below ground level, east of today's Damascus Gate. The lower portions of the wall are here built with stones typical of those used by Herod the Great, but they were probably reused by Herod Agrippa in his later construction of the northern wall of the city. The rebuilt arch over the gate has been dated to the time of the Roman emperor Hadrian in the second century.

Herod's family tomb?
Although Herod the Great was buried in Herodium, near Bethlehem, portions of a stone structure recently discovered beneath modern Arab housing north-west of the Damascus Gate in Jerusalem may be Herod's family tomb. The structure is round, with concentric walls, similar in style to the unique architecture of Herod the Great in Israel – seen for example in the circular palace/fortress of Herodium and in the round structure in the middle of his pool there; in the round pavilion in Herod's northern palace at Masada; and in the round structure in his bathhouse at Jericho. The tomb's style is similar to the Tomb of Augustus in Rome, which may have served as its model. There is no evidence to support the identification of the Roman-type tomb adjacent to the King David Hotel in Jerusalem, popularly known as 'the tomb of the Herods', as belonging to Herod's family.

Herodian Structures outside Jerusalem

Apart from Jerusalem, Herod the Great was a lavish builder, involved in construction projects at 20 sites within his kingdom and 13 outside its borders. He built a number of palaces in the deserts of Judea that functioned as both fortresses and as comfortable living quarters when he was travelling.

Herodium

Herod built a palace/fortress surrounded by two circular walls with four towers on a hill at Herodium, about 5 kilometres (3 miles) southeast of Bethlehem. Within its walls, Herodium boasted living quarters, a courtyard, dining hall, bathhouse and five large cisterns, four of them underground.

At the foot of the hill, Herod built a lower palace on an 18-hectare (45-acre) site; the palace comprised a residence, large causeway, monumental building and a magnificent garden containing a huge colonnaded pool with a circular island in the middle. When Herod died in Jericho, he was taken to Herodium for burial. An Israeli archaeologist claimed that he discovered the tomb in 2007.

Jericho

In Jericho, 22 kilometres (14 miles) east of Jerusalem, Herod built another large palace complex, comprising residential quarters, two swimming pools, a sunken garden, reception hall, courtyard and Roman bath. In the residential quarters six *mikvaot* (Jewish ritual baths) have been excavated – the earliest so far found in Israel – along with other pools and even stone bathtubs.

Masada

A third desert palace/fortress was built by Herod at Masada on the west side of the Dead Sea, about

Left: Herodium
Below: Inside the cone at the top of Herodium.

Above: Colonnaded pool with circular island at foot of Herodium.
Right: Excavations at Herodian Jericho.

48 kilometres (30 miles) south of its northern end. Masada is an isolated butte rising 420 metres (1,380 feet) above the surface level of the Dead Sea. Its flat top is 580 metres (1,900 feet) from north to south and 305 metres (1,000 feet) from east to west at its widest point. Herod built over previously existing structures dating to the second century B.C. and added some of his own unique construction.

A double wall with 110 towers and with partitions 4 metres (13 feet) wide was constructed around the perimeter of Masada, with a three-tiered palace on its northern slopes. South of this, Herod built a public bathhouse, with an administrative centre to its west, and in the middle of the fortress, along the western edge of the butte, a western palace, with a large swimming pool or bath near its south-east corner.

In the western wall of Masada was found a synagogue that was probably constructed by Zealots during the occupation of Masada in the years immediately before the fall of Jerusalem in A.D. 70. This synagogue is one of the three oldest synagogues so far discovered in Israel (the other two are at Herodium and Gamla).

The Cave of Machpelah
Herod built a monumental wall in Hebron around the Cave of

Machpelah, where Abraham, Isaac, Jacob and their wives, Sarah, Rebekah and Leah, were buried. (The tomb of Rachel, another wife of Jacob, is in Bethlehem.) The beautifully carved Herodian stone is still preserved in the wall around Machpelah, with a design identical to that which Herod used in the enclosure wall of the Temple Mount in Jerusalem.

Caesarea
One of Herod's greatest successes was the city of Caesarea Maritima, on the coast of Israel, halfway between modern Tel-Aviv and Haifa. Unlike other cities with which he was involved, Herod built this 66-hectare (164-acre) city from scratch on a completely new site, naming it Caesarea in honour of Caesar (Augustus). Herod built here the first artificial harbour in

the ancient world – even larger than the harbour of Athens, Piraeus. The Herodian harbour was much larger than the later Crusader one now standing; part of its breakwater walls can still be seen beneath the surface, and excavations on the shore have uncovered portions of the dock and many warehouses.

Foundations of a temple Herod built in honour of the emperor Augustus and of Roma, the goddess of Rome, have been found on a terrace east of the harbour at Caesarea. This is one of three temples that the first-century Jewish historian Josephus said Herod built in Israel in honour of Augustus, the other two being in Caesarea Philippi and Samaria.

A few hundred metres south of the harbour at Caesarea Maritima, recent excavations have uncovered the

promontory palace of Herod, with a nearby pool. And, very recently, a stadium Herod built was uncovered adjacent to the north side of the palace. This was 300 metres (960 feet) long and 50 metres (164 feet) wide, and may have had as many as 15,000 seats.

Adjacent to the palace and the stadium at Caesarea there is a Roman theatre, which is probably a reconstruction of an earlier stadium built by Herod. A stone, originally part of the nearby temple honouring the emperor Tiberius (A.D. 14–37), was found reused in a step of this theatre. It has a dedicatory Latin inscription that states:

PONTIUS PILATE PREFECT OF JUDEA HAS DEDICATED TO THE PEOPLE OF CAESAREA A TEMPLE IN HONOUR OF TIBERIUS.

This is the first and only reference to Pilate – the Prefect of Judea (A.D. 26–36) under whom Jesus was crucified – found in archaeological excavations.

In A.D. 44, an occasion recorded in Acts (12:20–23), Herod Agrippa I put on his royal robes, took his seat on his throne and spoke to the people, an event Josephus locates in the theatre. Josephus goes on to say that as soon as Herod accepted the people's acclamation as a god, he was struck with a severe ailment ('eaten by worms' Acts 12:23), was carried from the theatre and died within five days (*Antiquities, 19.344–50*).

An inscription found in 1997 on a mosaic floor at Caesarea has been identified as part of the Roman bureau for internal security, where Paul appeared before Festus

Top: Masada.
Above left: Part of the three-tiered palace at Masada.
Above: Inscription in floor of Roman Internal Security Office.

(Acts 24:27; 25:1–6). The inscription reads 'I came to this office – I shall be secure.' The building complex where it was found includes a large palace, administrative offices, a bathhouse and a courtyard.

A substantial section of the impressive aqueduct which Herod constructed on Roman arches to supply Caesarea with water still stands north of the city. It once brought water from a source about 14 kilometres (9 miles) north-east of Caesarea.

Jesus' Youth and Ministry in Galilee and Judea

Nazareth
The traditional spot of the angel Gabriel's annunciation to Mary of the coming birth of Jesus (Luke 1:26–27) is marked by the modern Church of the Annunciation in the heart of the city of Nazareth, which was only a small village when Jesus lived and worked there for thirty years. Beneath this huge church are some remains of an ancient dwelling which Christian tradition connects with Joseph and Mary.

Bethlehem
The traditional birthplace of Jesus, in a cave in Bethlehem, is marked by the Church of the Nativity, constructed by the sixth-century emperor Justinian over the remains of a fourth-century church built by Helena, the mother of the emperor Constantine. Remains of Helena's church can still be seen inside the present building.

Due to the scarcity of wood and hence the expense of constructing stables, it was normal in the Holy Land to build houses above caves which could be used as animal stables. Both Justin Martyr in the second century and Origen in the third wrote of a cave beneath the Church of the Nativity as being the place where Jesus was born. This cave, which today is beneath the apse at the east end of the Church of the Nativity, has a silver star inlaid into a marble pavement to mark the spot venerated for centuries as the birthplace of Jesus.

Capernaum
When Jesus was rejected at Nazareth, he went to Capernaum (Luke 4:16, 29–31) on the north shore of the Sea of Galilee, probably staying in the home of Simon Peter (Matthew 8:14–16). Excavations in Capernaum have revealed the remains of a fifth-century chapel built over a house which had been venerated since the middle of the first century, leading archaeologists to believe it to be the house of Peter.

Parts of the stone floor and walls of a first-century synagogue have been discovered beneath the fourth-century synagogue in Capernaum. This was probably the same synagogue where Jesus taught (Luke 4:33, 38), since Capernaum was a small village and likely had only one synagogue.

Tiberias
Excavations in the southern part of the city of Tiberias, built on the western shore of the Sea of Galilee to honour Tiberius Caesar, have revealed portions of a stone-paved road and a city gate, with two circular stone towers south of the gate, each 7 metres (23 feet) in diameter, all of which were constructed by Herod Antipas (4 B.C.–A.D. 39). Recent excavations in Tiberias have also uncovered a stadium built by Antipas.

Gergesa
The place where Jesus cast the demons out of a man and sent them into a herd of pigs that ran over a 'steep bank into the sea' (Mark 5:13) is probably El Kursi (ancient Gergesa),

Church of the Annunciation in Nazareth.

Above: Church of the Nativity in Bethlehem.
Left: Synagogue in Capernaum.
Below left: Part of reconstructed synagogue, Capernaum.

the only place on the eastern shore of the Sea of Galilee where the cliff comes out to the sea. Above the city, a number of caves and tombs have been found, as described in the Gospels, which say the man possessed by demons was living among tombs (Mark 5:5). A sixth-century Byzantine church was built here, probably to commemorate this event.

Bethsaida

Excavations since 1995 on the northern shore of the Sea of Galilee have uncovered the remains of a city which archaeologists have identified as Bethsaida, where Jesus fed the crowd with five loaves and two fish (Luke 9:10–17). This site lies 2.5 kilometres (1.5 miles) north of the present shore of the Sea of Galilee, but the sea extended further north in the time of Jesus.

Sepphoris

After the death of Herod the Great, his son Herod Antipas became ruler of Galilee and built the impressive city of Sepphoris only 6.5 kilometres (4 miles)

north of Nazareth. Excavations conducted there since 1983 have uncovered remains of the city, including a theatre probably built by Herod Antipas. Joseph, Jesus' earthly father, was a carpenter, and since the city was so close to Nazareth, he and Jesus may have worked on its construction, though Sepphoris is not mentioned in the New Testament.

Cana

Jesus performed his first miracle, turning water into wine, at a marriage in Cana of Galilee (John 2:11). Current excavations at Khirbet Cana ('Ruins of Cana'), 14 kilometres (9 miles) north of Nazareth, are building a case for identifying it with the Cana of Jesus' miracle. There is no archaeological or historical evidence to support the tradition that the modern village of Kefr Cana (Arabic for 'City of Cana'), 8 kilometres (5 miles) north-east of Nazareth, is the Cana mentioned in John's Gospel.

Caesarea Philippi

The ruins of a magnificent palace of Herod Agrippa II have been excavated at Caesarea Philippi, in northern Israel, where Jesus told Peter 'on this rock I will build my church' (Matthew 16:18). Excavated remains there include portions of a reception hall, a public bathhouse

Top: Chapel above possible site of Peter's house in Capernaum.
Above left: Site of El Kursi where the cliff comes out to the sea.
Above right: Caesarea Philippi.

and large circular towers that fortified the north–south colonnaded street running through the centre of the city.

Jesus' Ministry and Last Days in Judea

Sychar
On one occasion, when Jesus was passing through Samaria on his way from Judea to Galilee, he paused with his disciples to rest at Jacob's Well, near the village of Sychar (John 4:1–6), located slightly north-east of modern-day Nablus (Old Testament Shechem). There is a well in this area that might be the well where Jesus talked to the woman of Samaria about Jewish and Samaritan worship.

Mount Gerizim
During her conversation with Jesus, the woman said that her ancestors had 'worshipped on this mountain' – referring to Mount Gerizim, on the south side of the village of Shechem. The Samaritan temple that once stood on this mountain was destroyed more than a century before the time of Jesus.

Excavations on the summit of Mount Gerizim have recently uncovered the foundations of this temple, with portions of its walls, gates and altars and inscriptions written in ancient Hebrew. The Samaritan temple complex covered some 40 hectares (100 acres) and included living quarters for about 1,500 people.

Bethany
In the fourth century A.D., the Christian historian Eusebius described Bethany as 'a village at the second milestone from Aelia [Jerusalem], in a steep bank of the Mount of Olives, where Christ raised Lazarus. The place of Lazarus is being shown even until now.' This 'place' is a tomb which tradition assigns to the story of Lazarus. The original entrance to the tomb was on the east; the present entrance, on the north, was cut centuries later during the Muslim period.

The tomb is small, with a vestibule opening to the north through a narrow passage 1.5 metres (5 feet) long to the burial chamber, which is about 2.5 metres (8 feet) square. A church was built at the tomb in the fourth century A.D., but it was destroyed, probably by an earthquake, and rebuilt with modifications in the following centuries. The modern church, dedicated in 1954, stands over the ruins of the previous structures. There is no way conclusively to identify the tomb as that of Lazarus.

Left: Entrance to tomb of Lazarus in Bethany.
Below: Mount Gerizim and foundations of Samaritan Temple.

James inscription

In 2002 an antiquities dealer in Jerusalem brought to public attention an ossuary with an inscription in Aramaic on it which reads 'James, son of Joseph, brother of Jesus'. This was declared in *Time* magazine and in *Biblical Archaeology Review* to be the 'most important discovery in the history of New Testament archaeology'. But whether it is in fact the burial box of the brother of Jesus of Nazareth cannot be proved scientifically.

Pool of Bethesda

Excavations in Jerusalem have revealed a twin pool with porches. This may be the Pool of Bethesda, where Jesus healed an invalid (John 5:1f). Two large pools have been excavated about 90 metres (100 yards) north of the Temple Mount's northern wall. Cut into rock and plastered, these pools lie close to the west side of the Church of Saint Anne.

Siloam Pool

Excavations at the southern end of Hezekiah's Tunnel, south of the Temple Mount, have uncovered the eastern portion of a large pool, 50 metres (165 feet) long (its width is not yet known), lying only about 10 metres (32 feet) south of the little pool long identified as the Siloam Pool. These are undoubtedly part of a large complex called the Siloam Pool (which, like the Pool of Bethesda, had two sections), where Jesus healed a blind man by having him wash his eyes in its water (John 9:1–41).

Caiaphas' family tomb

An ancient burial cave which belonged to the family of Caiaphas, the high priest who interrogated Jesus and then delivered him to the Roman governor Pontius Pilate (Matthew 26:57—27:2), has been found in the Peace Forest, about 1.5 kilometres (1 mile) south of the Old City of Jerusalem. One of the ossuaries in this cave had the name of 'Joseph, son of Caiaphas' carved twice on it. Inside the ossuary were the bones of six people, including those of a man of about 60, which may well be those of Caiaphas.

Jesus' burial place

A tomb inside the Church of the Holy

Top left: Pool of Bethesda.
Above: Siloam Pool.
Above left: Tomb of Caiaphas.

Sepulchre in Jerusalem's Old City is probably the burial place of Jesus. Queen Helena, the mother of the emperor Constantine, erected the church here in the fourth century on the basis of a long-standing tradition that this was where Jesus was buried.

The Garden Tomb

The Garden Tomb, north of Jerusalem's Damascus Gate, has also been considered a possible site of Jesus' burial. It is cut into a cliff side, and is part of two large burial sites near St Stephen's Church that belong to the École Biblique, the French School of Archaeology. But the tombs in this burial ground all date to the Iron Age, 1,200 years before Christ, and the Garden Tomb is a part of this ancient tomb complex.

Cities of Paul in Asia Minor

Asia Minor (the modern country of Turkey) is a primary location in New Testament history. Much of the Apostle Paul's travels were in this area.

Tarsus

Paul was born a Roman citizen in the city of Tarsus (Acts 22:27–28), which lay on the Cydnus River, about 16 kilometres (10 miles) north of the south-east coast of Asia Minor (Turkey). Along with Alexandria and Athens, Tarsus was one of the three most important educational centres of the Mediterranean world at this period. Tarsus has been only briefly excavated, and nothing significant was found from the Roman period. Roman Tarsus still lies buried beneath the surface of the modern city.

Damascus

Paul was converted to Christ on the road to Damascus in Syria, where the street of Paul's day, called 'Straight Street' (Acts 9:11) probably lies beneath a main street of the modern city. It was a 15-metre (50-foot) wide colonnaded street, and some of its columns have been excavated while others still stand amid the modern shops. Remains of a theatre, a monumental Roman arch and a possible palace have been found along this street.

Antioch of Syria

After his conversion, and some years in Arabia, the Apostle Paul made Antioch of Syria the headquarters for his work. This Graeco-Roman city, which in the first century A.D. had a population of probably about 300,000, played a larger part in the history of the early church than any other city except Jerusalem. It was here that the term 'Christian' was first used for the disciples of Jesus (Acts 11:26); yet there are few archaeological remains in the city from the time of Paul.

Salamis

Paul, accompanied by Barnabas, began his first missionary journey by leaving Antioch to sail to the island of Cyprus, where he preached in the synagogue in the city of Salamis, 8 kilometres (5 miles) from the modern city of Famagusta (Acts 13:5).

**Left: Sergius Paulus inscription, Yalvaç.
Below: Theatre at Salamis.**

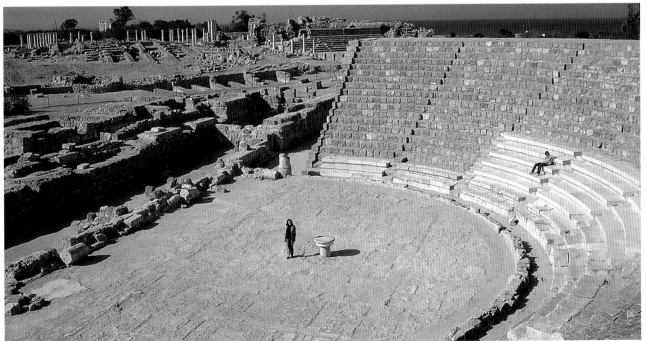

Remains of a Roman theatre dating to the end of the first century B.C. may still be seen in Salamis, near the gymnasium and palestra (exercising area), which is surrounded by marble columns with Corinthian capitals.

Paphos

Paul also visited the town of Paphos on the west coast of Cyprus (Acts 13:6–7), which had an excellent harbour. Here he converted the Roman proconsul Sergius Paulus to Christ. The family of this Roman official came from near Antioch of Pisidia, in central Asia Minor, and Paul's decision to go on to Asia Minor might have been influenced by this official's wanting Paul to talk to his family about the gospel. An inscription displayed in the Yalvaç Museum, near Antioch of Pisidia, has the name of Sergius Paulus carved on it.

Perga

Paul sailed from Paphos to Perga, a port city up the river Cestrus from the southern coast of Asia Minor (Acts 13:13). Perga boasts impressive archaeological remains, including a large Roman forum or marketplace, city walls and towers, twin horseshoe-shaped gates through which Paul would have entered the city from the south, a Graeco-Roman type of theatre and a well-preserved stadium.

Antioch of Pisidia

Paul proclaimed the gospel in Antioch of Pisidia (home of Sergius Paulus), located in central Asia Minor (Acts 13:14; 14:21). Remains of a temple to Augustus have been excavated there, and finds include portions of a Latin

inscription dating from the time when Paul and Barnabas were in the city. This inscription is of considerable importance for the history of that period.

Attalia

At the end of his first missionary journey, Paul sailed out of Attalia (modern Antalya), which is still a major harbour on the southern coast of Turkey (Acts 14:25). From here, Roman roads led throughout Asia Minor, and from such a major hub Paul could find coast-hopping vessels to various ports on the Mediterranean Sea.

Troas and Assos

Paul extended his second missionary journey into western Asia Minor. The best evidence available for the city of Troas, which has few archaeological remains, is from coins. The city of Assos, 48 kilometres (30 miles) south of Troas, was built on the coast, with a small harbour from which Paul sailed to Miletus (Acts 20:14–15). The modern

Top left: Miletus Gate in Pergamum Museum in Berlin.
Top right: Excavations of Temple of Augustus at Antioch.
Above left: Horseshoe gate, Perga.
Above: Theatre at Miletus.

harbour is built on the site of the ancient one. On a hill above the city, ruins of the ancient Temple of Athena still look down upon the harbour.

Miletus

On the return segment of his third missionary journey, Paul visited Miletus (Acts 20:17ff). Among the most impressive remains of the ancient city is the marketplace whose monumental gate was dismantled in the nineteenth century, taken to the Pergamum Museum in Berlin and reassembled. The theatre still standing in Miletus contains some of the best preserved hallways among ancient theatres.

Asia Minor in the Book of Revelation

Patmos

On the Aegean island of Patmos, 105 kilometres (65 miles) west of Ephesus in the Aegean Sea, John received his revelation, which included messages to churches in seven cities of western Asia Minor (modern Turkey). The Book of Revelation is addressed to these seven churches.

According to tradition, John's revelation was given in a cave behind an eleventh-century monastery on Ayios Elias, a 250-metre (800-foot) summit on the southern half of the island. Some have thought that John may have been exiled to Patmos to work in mines, but no archaeological evidence of ancient mining has been found. However, iron-bearing rocks have been discovered, and there are records of mining in modern times.

After his experience of exile, John spent his final years in Ephesus, where the Apostle Paul had also lived and worked for about two years (Acts 19:10). Beginning with Ephesus, the cities addressed in the letters of Revelation 1–3 are arranged in the order of an ancient postal route, which ran clockwise from the coast inland.

Smyrna

The only part of the city of Smyrna (modern Izmir) that has been excavated is the ancient forum (marketplace). This consisted of a rectangular piazza, bordered on two sides – perhaps three – by two-storied triple porticoes (colonnaded porches). The north side was occupied by a huge basilica, also with two stories.

On the west end of the forum was a rostrum (public speaker's platform), and beneath it ran a magnificent vaulted basement, whose arched ceilings supported the floor of the marketplace above. The forum area was also covered with inscriptions of various periods. Unfortunately, almost nothing of the New Testament city is still standing.

Pergamum

The invention of parchment (that is, specially treated animal skin) is attributed to the city of Pergamum, and the Greek and Latin word, *pergamena,* translated into English as 'parchment', comes from the name 'Pergamum'. Some of the oldest copies of the New Testament were written on parchment.

A huge marble altar of Zeus stood on the mountain top at Pergamum and has been partially reconstructed

Left: The ancient forum, Smyrna.
Below: Island of Patmos.

in the Pergamum Museum in Berlin. This altar is considered by some scholars to be 'the throne of Satan' referred to in the letter to the church at Pergamum (Rev. 2:13). However, the Book of Revelation was evidently written in the context of emperor worship (the Imperial Cult), and it is more likely that Pergamum's Temple of Augustus, the first provincial temple built to a Roman emperor in Asia Minor, was the 'throne of Satan'. This Temple of Augustus has not yet been identified in the excavations, but some coins minted in Pergamum portray the temple on one side and the head of Augustus on the other.

An impressive theatre with 10,000 seats was built on the mountainside at Pergamum, overlooking the Caicus Valley. It was erected in the third century B.C., renovated in the Roman period, and was functioning at the time that Revelation was written.

Sardis
From Thyatira, where little of archaeological importance remains, the postal route ran on to Sardis, which is also largely unexcavated. A post-fourth-century synagogue has been found, beneath which is evidence of a first-century synagogue and other remains from the Hellenistic and Roman levels which date back to the time of John. Parts of the walls and columns of the Temple of Artemis and portions of a marble road that ran through the city have also been excavated.

Laodicea
Although Philadelphia still remains unexcavated, excavations at Laodicea since 2003 have revealed portions of a city wall, a monumental street, a Greek and Roman theatre and a small Roman *odeion* (recital hall).

Top: Temple of Artemis at Sardis.
Middle: Altar of Zeus at Pergamum.
Bottom: Arched ceilings of vaulted basement in Smyrna.

Ephesus

In Paul's time, Ephesus was a city of about 200,000 people, whose commerce, trade guilds and banking capacities gave it pre-eminent importance. Extensive excavations have revealed the impressive remains of well-preserved streets paved with stone, a civic forum and a commercial marketplace, with some shops still intact on its south side. It was in shops such as these that Paul worked as a leather-worker with Priscilla and Aquila in Corinth (Acts 18:2–4) and perhaps in Ephesus too.

Ephesus was laid out around two hills. Its main thoroughfare was made up of several sections: beginning as Curetes Street at the Magnesian Gate in the east, proceeding west to the lower marketplace, where it turned north and became the 'Marble Road'. This portion of the street then ran the full length of the east side of the marketplace, past the theatre. In front of the theatre it became 'Stadion Street', continuing on northwards.

The Arcadian Way, another major colonnaded thoroughfare – 11 metres (36 feet) wide and almost 610 metres (2,000 feet) long – ran westwards to the harbour, which has long since silted up.

The theatre

The theatre mentioned in Acts 19:22 is still standing. It is almost 30 metres (100 feet) high and would have seated 24,000 people, being the largest theatre in the ancient world, and the only one to have seven entrances on to its stage. John's constant use of the number seven in his dramatic images in Revelation may have been prompted by his readers' familiarity with this stage.

As we have noticed, John spent his last years in Ephesus, and the Book of Revelation is set against the background of provincial Asia at this time. John may have adapted the genre of Greek tragedy as performed in this theatre to present his Patmos vision, and may have written Revelation as though the dramatic revelation he received were being acted out on this stage.

Artemis

Partial remains have been found of the office of the town clerk who went to the theatre adjacent to its north

Left: Commercial Agora in Ephesus.
Below left: The Arcadian Way in Ephesus.
Below: Curetes Street in Ephesus.

side to pacify the mob gathered there shouting in protest against Paul's attack on their idols (Acts 19:35). The protest was based on the loss of income by silversmiths, who were selling fewer silver images of Artemis (the Roman goddess Diana) as a result of Paul's successful preaching. Two beautifully sculpted statues of Artemis, excavated in the town hall, are displayed in the museum in nearby Seljuk.

Villas

The most recent discoveries in Ephesus are in the housing complex on the south side of the main road. Excavations have revealed that wealthy and middle-class people were living near one another in luxurious villas and high-rise apartments.

The interiors of some of these villas testify to the wealth in the city, and would have been big enough to allow Christians to assemble in them as 'house churches' for study and worship. (Dedicated church buildings were not allowed in the Roman Empire until 300 years later.) Paul's friends among the wealthy, influential and powerful Roman political officials here, men Luke calls 'Asiarchs', may have lived in such homes. It was some of these Asiarchs who persuaded Paul to stay out of the theatre during the demonstration (Acts 19:31).

Top: Theatre in Ephesus.
Above left: Interior of Roman villa in Ephesus.
Above: Statue of Artemis in Seljuk.

Inscriptions found in Ephesus show that 106 Asiarchs are known to have been in the city.

Macedonian Cities

When Paul extended his missionary work from Asia to Europe, he sailed from Troas to the island of Samothrace, where there was an important pagan place of worship dedicated to the gods of the Samothracian mystery religion.

Impressive foundations of this building have been excavated. Paul and his companions spent the night at Samothrace, before continuing their journey the next day. There was no Jewish synagogue on the island, and Paul was responding to the heavenly call to go on to Macedonia (Acts 16:9–12).

Neapolis

They next sailed direct to Neapolis in Macedonia (Acts 16:11), where remains of the ancient harbour still survive. A museum in the city contains in its yard milestones that once stood beside the Egnatian Way, the international Roman highway that passed through.

Philippi

Paul would have travelled the Egnatian Way to get to Philippi (Acts 16:12). Portions of the stone-surfaced Roman road have been excavated in the centre of Philippi next to the north side of the Roman forum (Acts 16:19).

Excavations at Philippi have produced paving stones and part of a stone platform (tribunal) in the north side of the forum, where Paul and Silas were arrested, beaten and dragged before the city magistrates (Acts 16:19–23).

On the north side of the forum, the other side of the Egnatian Way, is a small stone building which, since the fifth century, has been identified as the prison where Paul was held.

Left: Harbour at Neapolis.
Below: Sanctuary of the Great Gods, Samothrace.

However, this structure may not have been big enough to have constituted the 'inner prison' of the larger complex mentioned in Acts 16:24.

A theatre built about the time the city of Philippi was founded, and remodelled into a Roman theatre in the second century A.D., was standing when Paul was here. The current seats are not original, but were restored in the 1950s.

Thessalonica

Paul's arrival in Thessalonica (Acts 17:1) put him in the capital city of the second district of Macedonia. Coins had begun to be minted in Macedonia under Claudius (A.D. 41–54), about the time that Paul arrived (late autumn A.D. 49), and prosperity was everywhere evident. Among Paul's converts here were 'Greek women of high standing' (Acts 17:12) who took their place in a society that boasted great families possessing huge wealth.

When Macedonia became a Roman province in 146 B.C., Thessalonica became its capital. It was beautifully situated, at the head of the Thermaic Gulf, with a large commercial harbour and, occupying an important position on the Egnatian Road, it became a cultural centre of international repute where poets and philosophers

addressed cultured audiences.

Systematic excavations have been carried out during which a typical rectangular forum with a paved court and small theatre were uncovered. The court was surrounded by a portico beneath which, on the south side, was a double subterranean porch (*cryptoporticus*), similar to that at Smyrna in Asia Minor.

Archaeology has made a positive contribution to a problem about Thessalonica that has been hotly disputed for many years. Critics of the New Testament have claimed

Top: Philippi forum, looking east.
Bottom: Prison of Paul, Philippi.

Luke was mistaken in his use of the term 'Politarchs' for the officials before whom Paul was taken in this city, because there was no evidence that such an office existed. However, 35 inscriptions have been discovered using this term, 19 of them from Thessalonica, 3 of the latter from the first century A.D. One inscription containing this term was discovered on an arch at the west end of the modern street called Odos Egnatia, and is now

Beroea

From Thessalonica, Paul travelled on to Beroea, where today there is a museum full of fine Roman statues, inscriptions and funerary altars, which overflow into a congested courtyard. One of the first-century Politarch inscriptions mentioned above was found in Beroea.

Another Greek inscription found in this city contains 'The Gymnasiarchal Law of Beroea', which lists three categories of people who play in the gymnasium, with their ages:

on display in the British Museum, London. The inscription begins, 'In the time of the Politarchs . . . ' Archaeology has now made it incontrovertible that 'Politarchs' existed in Macedonia during the time of the Apostle Paul.

Top: Theatre in Philippi.
Left: Inscription in yard of museum in Thessalonica.
Above: Square, *cryptoporticus*, theatre at Thessalonica.

1. *Paides* – up to age 15
2. *Epheboi* – ages 15–17
3. *Neoi* or *neaniskoi* – ages 18–22.

This third group may provide some indication of the age of Timothy, who is referred to as a 'youth ' (*neotes*) in 1 Timothy 4:12.

Athens

Athens was one of the most interesting and well-known cities of the ancient world. Unlike the largest cities of that time, such as Antioch of Syria, Ephesus, Alexandria, Rome and even Corinth, Athens was a relatively small university town, of about 25,000 people. More concerned with ideas than commerce, it lived on the memory of its glorious past.

The Parthenon
On arriving in Athens, the Apostle Paul would doubtless have admired the splendour of the architecture, evident in the Parthenon on the Acropolis (a rocky hill) – but he felt revulsion when he saw the polytheism and pagan idolatry Athens had represented for half a millennium.

Passing through the entrance gate of the Acropolis, Paul would have gazed upon the Parthenon (temple of Athena). In 1687, when the Venetians were attempting to take Athens from the Turks, this monumental building, which had been turned into a storage depot for ammunition, was hit by a mortar shell and badly damaged.

The Parthenon in its glory is best visualized by the replica built in 1931 in Nashville, Tennessee. The original sculpture of Athena Parthenos, the goddess of wisdom, prudent warfare and the arts, was created by Phidias in the fifth century B.C. The replica in the Nashville Parthenon, completed in 1992, recreates the size and colour

of the original. Standing almost 13 metres (42 feet) tall, it is the largest piece of indoor sculpture in the modern Western world.

As already mentioned, another temple on the Acropolis of importance to students of New Testament archaeology is the Temple of Roma and Augustus, portions of which remain, just east of the Parthenon.

Above: Parthenon in Nashville, Tennessee, U.S.A.

Overall: The Acropolis, Athens, Greece.

Above: Tower of the Winds in Roman market in Athens.
Above right: Greek market in Athens with Stoa of Attalos in background.
Right: Mars Hill in foreground with Acropolis in background.

The agora

Paul carried on discussions daily in the agora, the Greek marketplace. There were both a Greek market and a Roman market, or forum, in Athens at the period when Paul visited the city. The western (Greek) market lay due north of Mars Hill and contained the prominent Temple of Hephaestus and Stoa of Attalos, where poets and philosophers met to walk together and talk. The Stoic philosophers, whom Paul addressed on Mars Hill, got their name from meeting on this stoa (or porch).

The agora square was kept free of public and private buildings alike for almost 500 years, but with the arrival of the Romans, in the reign of Augustus, the public square began to be filled with buildings and monuments, and there was almost no political activity there after the birth of Jesus.

Paul, however, probably spent most of his time in the commercial Roman market to the east, which had been started in the reign of Julius Caesar and was completed by Augustus. By contrast with the Greek market, this would have been alive with everyday business activity, and Paul would more likely have found the ear of the ordinary Athenian here.

The Roman market contains one of the best-preserved ancient monuments in Greece, a tall octagonal marble tower called 'The Tower of the Winds', a huge water clock, sundial and weathervane combined. Paul could have checked the time of day by this clock while teaching in the forum.

The Areopagus

While preaching in this agora, Paul was arrested and taken before the city officials, known as the 'Areopagus'. Since Paul had been speaking about 'foreign divinities', he fell under the jurisdiction of the Areopagus council, which had 'surveillance over the introduction of foreign divinities'. The traditional meeting place of the Areopagus was on Mars Hill, west of the Acropolis. (The god of war was called Ares by the Greeks – hence 'Areopagus' – and Mars by the Romans.)

Paul left Athens after a surprisingly brief stay, disappointed perhaps by limited success among both Greek intellectuals and the godfearers and Jews in the synagogue (Acts 17:17).

Corinth

In the first century A.D., the city of Corinth had a population of almost 1 million people, including slaves, and its walls extended for some 10 kilometres (6 miles) around the city.

Temple of Aphrodite

In the years preceding Paul's visit to Corinth in A.D. 49, a pagan Temple of Aphrodite stood on a nearby hill, called the Acrocorinth. Strabo, a first-century author, wrote of the immorality prevalent in the city, and stated that this temple owned 1,000 male and female temple-slaves or prostitutes dedicated to the goddess. Excavators have found evidence of the temple's foundations, and estimated it was no larger than 10 by 16 metres (33 by 52 feet). Since the temple was so small, and assuming Strabo's estimate to be correct, the large number of sacred prostitutes must have lived and functioned below, in the city of Corinth itself. Certainly Paul spoke of the prevalent fornication in Corinth (1 Corinthians 7:2).

Temple of Apollo

Nearer the agora, and standing on a high promontory, was the Temple of Apollo, one of the oldest in Greece, which had been restored by the time of Paul's visit. Seven Doric columns from this structure are still standing.

During the reign of Augustus, a series of shops was built along the western terrace of the marketplace. Paul worked as a tent-maker in shops such as these.

The theatre

The theatre of Corinth, one of the city's most imposing structures, was located north-west of the forum, and was used not only for theatrical performances but also for large civic meetings. Renovated about five years before Paul arrived, it commanded a view of the slopes leading down to the Gulf of Corinth, and would have seated approximately 14,000 spectators in 55 rows of seats.

Temple of Apollo, Corinth.

Erastus

Also just before Paul's arrival, a 20-metre (62-foot) square area at the north-east corner of the theatre area was paved with stone. In 1929, in an excavated part of this pavement, a slab of grey limestone was found on which was part of a Latin inscription in letters 18 centimetres (7 inches) high. Two other parts of the adjoining right slab containing the rest of the inscription were found in other parts of the theatre. The abbreviated Latin reads in full translation:

ERASTUS IN RETURN FOR HIS AEDILESHIP LAID [THE PAVEMENT] AT HIS OWN EXPENSE.

The Erastus of this inscription has been identified as the Erastus mentioned by Paul in his letter to the Romans. The reference is in Romans 16:23, a letter written from Corinth, where Paul writes: 'Erastus, the city treasurer, salutes you.'

The Bema

One of the most important discoveries at Corinth relating to the New Testament is the Bema, the speaker's platform, from which official proclamations were read

and where citizens appeared before appropriate officials. Paul stood here before Gallio in the summer of A.D. 51 (Acts 18:12–17).

The floor of the platform on which Gallio stood was at the same elevation as the terrace of the South Stoa behind it, while Paul would have stood about 2.25 metres (7.5 feet) below on a stone pavement built on to the north side of the platform, and at the level of the lower forum. The Bema was identified by several pieces of an inscription found nearby and

Top: Corinth from Acrocorinth.
Above: Acrocorinth.

dated to the period between A.D. 25 and 50, just before Paul's arrival in the city.

Top: Remains of the Temple of Aphrodite
on the Acrocorinth.
Above: Bema in Corinth.
Left: Erastus inscription in Corinth.

Rome

The forum
Rome was built on seven hills, with its forum, located between the Palatine and the Esquiline Hills, forming both the chief marketplace and the civic centre, where people came to conduct commercial, civic and religious affairs.

Augustus
In 29 B.C., Augustus dedicated a triumphal arch at the east end of the Roman forum built in honour of his naval victory at Actium two years earlier; it was subsequently replaced by a triple arch commissioned in 19 B.C. Adjacent to the north side of Caesar's forum, Augustus also built the Forum of Augustus, which contained a Temple of Mars at its northern end, and the massive imperial residence on the Palatine Hill, with a Temple of Apollo on its north side.

In the Campus Martius, on the east bank of the Tiber, the still partially-preserved Theatre of Marcellus was built. After Augustus returned from his victorious campaigns in Gaul and Spain, it was decreed in 14 B.C. that an Altar of Peace should be constructed here; this was completed and inaugurated in A.D. 9.

The Pantheon
The Mausoleum of Augustus was also erected in the same area, together with many other impressive temples and bathhouses, including the Pantheon (a temple to all the Roman gods).

This beautifully preserved structure, originally built by Augustus' architect, Agrippa, between 27 and 25 B.C., was completely rebuilt by the emperor Hadrian between A.D. 120 and 125. It stands today as a sample of the building activity of an emperor renowned for his construction programmes throughout the empire.

Vespasian's Arch
Historic arches are found in the forum and throughout the city of Rome. Only a few years after Paul came to Rome and was martyred (c. A.D. 67 or 68), the Roman Senate built an arch to honour the capture of Jerusalem in A.D. 70 by the general Titus. It stood in a prominent position at the south end of the forum, with the road into the forum passing under it. Titus was son of the Roman emperor Vespasian, and in time became emperor himself.

A carving within the arch depicts the Roman army carrying off the menorah (lampstand) from the Jerusalem Temple, adding archaeological credibility to the literary evidence of the Jewish War.

The Colosseum
The Colosseum, which would have seated about 45,000 people, stood on the south side of the forum and was one of the most impressive buildings in ancient Rome. It was called 'Colosseum' because of the colossal statue of the emperor Nero (A.D. 54–68) which stood nearby. It was begun by the emperor Vespasian (69–79) and completed by his sons,

Top: The Roman forum.
Bottom: Relief of menorah under Vespasian's Arch, Rome.

Above: Pantheon in Rome.
Left: Altar of Peace of Augustus in Rome.

Golden Milestone

At the west end of the Roman forum was the *Milliarium Aureum* (the Golden Milestone) from which were measured the distances to all the main cities of the empire. North of this stood the *Umbilicus Romae*, which marked the centre, not only of Rome, but also of the entire Roman world.

Church of St Paul

A church about 1.5 kilometres (1 mile) from the Gate of St Paul on the Via Ostiense is named the Church of St Paul Outside the Walls. No significant excavation has been done there, but tradition associates it with the death of Paul. The site is thought by some to be the location of a church commissioned by Constantine in the fourth century to replace an oratory (private chapel) built over the place where Lucina, a Roman matron, had buried Paul in her vineyard. When the present church was constructed, a marble slab was found under the altar that read *PAULO APOSTOLO MART[YRI]* in script characteristic of the time of Constantine.

Titus (79–81) and Domitian (81–96). Its external wall utilized the three basic patterns of Greek architecture in the form of columns with bases and capitals in the Doric, Ionic and Corinthian orders on the first, second and third stories respectively.

Some Christian martyrs died in this arena, but most were killed in the Circus Maximus, a short distance west of the Colosseum, between the Palatine and Aventine Hills.

Mammertine Prison

Near the Roman forum were two buildings that figured prominently in Paul's final imprisonment (2 Timothy 4:6–8). One was the Basilica Julia, built by Julius Caesar on the western side of the forum, where Paul may have heard his death sentence pronounced. The other (still standing) was the Mammertine Prison, at the foot of the Capitoline Hill, where Paul probably spent the last days of his life. In the sixteenth century a church called San Pietro in Carcere ('St Peter in prison') was built here, preserving a tradition that Peter was also imprisoned in the Mammertine Prison.

Ancient Documents

The discovery of ancient copies of the New Testament written on parchment, such as the Codex Vaticanus (fourth century) and the Codex Alexandrinus (fifth century) contributed significantly to our understanding of the history and transmission of the text of the Bible.

Codex Sinaiticus

In 1859, the German scholar Constantine von Tischendorf visited St Catherine's Monastery, at the foot of Mount Sinai, and made a discovery whose importance in some ways surpassed the publication that same year of Darwin's *Origin of Species*. A monk showed Tischendorf a copy of the Septuagint (a Greek translation of the Old Testament) in his possession. It was a fourth-century Greek manuscript containing most of the Old Testament and all of the New. This manuscript, now known as Codex Sinaiticus, is today on display in the British Library.

John Rylands Papyrus

The oldest part of any book of the New Testament yet found is P[52], the John Rylands Papyrus, discovered in 1920 in Egypt. This preserved fragment contains verses 31–33 of John 18 and dates to about A.D. 125.

This papyrus fragment and others, such as the Chester Beatty Papyrus of Paul's letters (P[46]), which is the earliest known copy of those letters (dating to about A.D. 200), have forced a re-evaluation of earlier studies that tried to date the composition of the Gospel of John and some of the Letters of Paul to the second century, giving additional support for the writing of all portions of the New Testament during the first century.

Hebrews

The study of these ancient documents has also shed light on the question of the authorship of the Letter to the Hebrews. In the Chester Beatty Papyrus, Hebrews is not only included in the corpus of Letters by Paul, but is placed second, behind Romans.

Below: A page of Bodmer III: John 11:31–37.
Bottom: The Isaiah Scroll from the Dead Sea Scrolls.

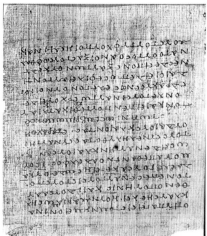

Romans 13:3 mosaic in Caesarea.

Furthermore, it is clear from the paragraph numbering system in *Codex Vaticanus* that the manuscript from which it was copied contained Hebrews among Paul's Letters. Galatians ends with paragraph number 58, but Ephesians begins with 70 – not 59. The first paragraph of Hebrews, which follows number 93 at the end of 2 Thessalonians, is numbered 59. It is obvious that an ancestor of Codex Vaticanus put the Letter to the Hebrews between Galatians and Ephesians.

The canon of the New Testament

These papyri have also given us an enriched perspective on our 27-document New Testament, which was not of course produced as a single volume. The Gospels, Acts, Letters and Revelation were written by various authors in several countries of the Mediterranean world over a period of 50 years and circulated separately for decades before being included in a single canon.

Codices

The longer books of the New Testament were probably written on codices (ancient books) rather than scrolls. Pagan documents were written on papyrus scrolls, while Jewish literature was produced on leather scrolls. Why Christians chose to use papyrus codices is unknown, but it may have been partially for economic reasons, because a scroll was written only on one side while the book form allowed writing on both sides of a sheet. Only 4 of the 88 known papyri are in scroll form; the remainder are codices.

The codex form also greatly simplified the search for passages within the document. The size of these documents in scroll form would have made their use burdensome. It is estimated that on a scroll about 38 centimetres (15 inches) high, the Letter of Paul to the Romans would be about 3.5 metres (12 feet) long. The Gospel of Mark, the shortest, would be about 6 metres (19 feet) long, while the Gospel of Luke would be about

10 metres (32 feet) long. The entire New Testament, if written on a single scroll, would have been more than 60 metres (200 feet) long! It would have been impossible to use, and as far as we know was never produced.

INDEX

Further reading
Alfred Hoerth and John
    McRay: *Bible Archaeology*
    (Baker, Grand Rapids,
    2005
James K. Hoffmeier: *The
    Archaeology of the Bible*
    (Lion, Oxford, 2008)
John McRay: *Archaeology
    and the New Testament*
    (Baker, Grand Rapids,
    1991)
John McRay: *Paul: His Life
    and Teaching* (Baker, Grand
    Rapids, 2003)

Copyright © 2008 Lion Hudson plc /
Tim Dowley Associates

Published in 2010 by Kregel Publications, a
division of Kregel, Inc., P.O. Box 2607, Grand
Rapids, Michigan 49501.

Worldwide co-edition produced by
Lion Hudson plc,
Wilkinson House, Jordan Hill Road,
Oxford OX2 8DR, England
Tel: +44 (0) 1865 302750
Fax: +44 (0) 1865 302757
Email: coed@lionhudson.com

ISBN 978-0-8254-3893-6
Printed in China

Photograph acknowledgments
All photographs by kind permission of
the author, except pp. 13 (reconstructed
synagogue), 18 (Horseshoe and Miletus),
and 32 (menorah), Tiger Design Ltd.